D1175870

Earthforms

Mountains

by Christine Webster

Consultant:
Robert S. Anderson, PhD
Associate Professor of Geological Sciences
University of Colorado at Boulder

Capstone
press

Mankato, Minnesota

Bridgestone Books are published by Capstone Press,
151 Good Counsel Drive, P.O. Box 669, Mankato, Minnesota 56002.
www.capstonepress.com

Copyright © 2005 by Capstone Press. All rights reserved.
No part of this publication may be reproduced in whole or in part, or stored in a retrieval
system, or transmitted in any form or by any means, electronic, mechanical, photocopying,
recording, or otherwise, without written permission of the publisher.
For information regarding permission, write to Capstone Press,
151 Good Counsel Drive, P.O. Box 669, Dept. R, Mankato, Minnesota 56002.
Printed in the United States of America

Library of Congress Cataloging-in-Publication Data
Webster, Christine.
    Mountains / by Christine Webster.
    p. cm.—(Bridgestone books. Earthforms)
    Includes bibliographical references and index.
    ISBN 0-7368-3714-0 (hardcover)
    1. Mountains—Juvenile literature. I. Title. II Series
GB512.W438 2005
910' .914'3—dc22
                                                            2004014278

Summary: Describes mountains, including how they form, plants and animals on mountains, how people
    and weather change mountains, mountains in North America, and Mount Everest.

Editorial Credits

Becky Viaene, editor; Juliette Peters, designer; Anne McMullen, map illustrator; Ted Williams,
    illustrator; Wanda Winch, photo researcher; Scott Thoms, photo editor

Photo Credits

Corbis/Alison Wright, 18; Sygma/Grazia Neri/Sestini, 12; Tibor Bognar, cover
James P. Rowan, 4, 8, 16
Photodisc/Alan and Sandy Carey, 10; PhotoLink, 1; PhotoLink/Kent Knudson, 14

1 2 3 4 5 6 10 09 08 07 06 05

Table of Contents

What Are Mountains?

Mountains are high points of land. They are like hills, but much taller. Mountains are taller than 1,000 feet (305 meters). They can have rounded tops or sharp **peaks**.

Some mountains stand alone. Most are grouped together with other mountains in a **mountain range**.

◄ Many tall, sharp peaks are found in the Swiss Alps mountain range.

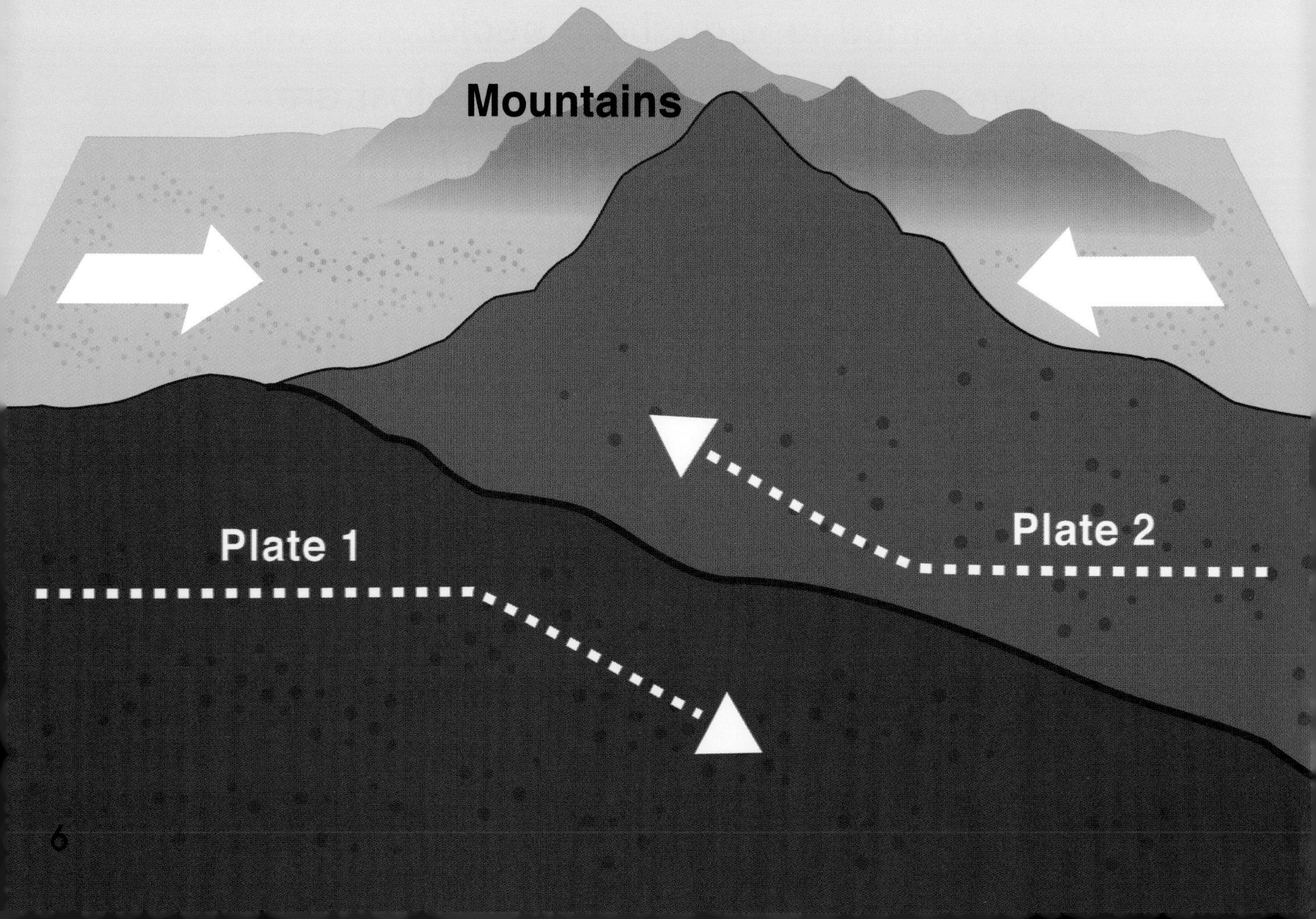

Mountains

Plate 1

Plate 2

How Do Mountains Form?

Mountains are often made by huge pieces of rock called plates. Plates make up earth's surface. The plates push against each other. When two plates bump into each other, one plate slides above the other. Land is pushed up. The Rocky Mountains in the United States formed this way.

Volcanoes also make mountains. Mountains form when lava comes out of earth's crust. The lava cools and hardens. More lava piles on top of it. A mountain slowly becomes taller.

◄ Mountains form when plates bump into each other. One plate slides above the other and pushes land up.

Plants on Mountains

On mountains, the **climate** changes as **elevation** increases. Different plants live on different elevations of mountains. Low areas are warmer. Oak and maple trees often grow at lower elevations. At higher, colder levels, pine and spruce trees grow.

Large plants cannot grow above a mountain's **tree line**. The weather is too cold. Only small shrubs and mosses grow above the tree line. No plants can live at the top of mountains with very cold climates.

◀ Spruce, pine, and fir trees are found below the tree line on mountains in Montana's Glacier National Park.

Animals on Mountains

Many animals live in warm areas below the tree line. Llamas make their homes on the Andes Mountains of South America. Grizzly bears are found below the tree line of the Rocky Mountains.

A few types of animals do live above the tree line. Mountain goats climb high on the Swiss Alps in Europe. Bighorn sheep are seen on the Rocky Mountains. Snow leopards live high on the Himalaya of Asia.

◄ Dall sheep live on Alaskan and Canadian mountains. They have smaller bodies and horns than bighorn sheep.

12

Weather Changes Mountains

Weather slowly **erodes** mountains. Rain and wind break rocks into small pieces. Sometimes rocks and dirt tumble down mountains in **landslides**. Weather can erode sharp mountain peaks into rounded tops.

Large bodies of ice called **glaciers** also change mountains. When weather warms up, glaciers slide down tall mountains slowly. They drag rocks and ice with them. Glaciers also cut deep valleys into mountains.

◀ A landslide from Mount Sarno ruins buildings in Italy.

People Change Mountains

People change mountains so they can travel on them. They build roads. They also make hiking and skiing trails.

People also change mountains when they cut down trees. Trees keep mountains from eroding. Without trees, rain can cause landslides. Many animals live in trees. When trees are cut, they have to find new homes.

◀ Each year, many mountain trees are cut down.

Mountains in North America

The Rocky Mountains are the largest mountain range in North America. They stretch about 3,000 miles (4,828 kilometers) from Canada to New Mexico.

The Appalachian Mountains reach from Canada into the United States. These mountains have eroded and are now shorter than the Rocky Mountains.

The Alaska Range lies in central Alaska. The highest mountain in North America is in this range. Mount Denali rises to 20,320 feet (6,194 meters).

◀ Deep valleys in Rocky Mountain National Park have been formed by glaciers.

Mount Everest

Mount Everest is the tallest mountain in the world. It is found in the Himalaya. Mount Everest reaches to 29,028 feet (8,848 meters).

At least 4,000 people have tried to climb Mount Everest. About 140 have died trying. About 660 people have made it to the top. Sir Edmund Hillary and Tenzing Norgay climbed Mount Everest in 1953. They were the first people to climb up and down safely.

◄ Mount Everest has rocky land, cold weather, and high winds.

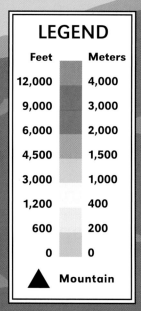

LEGEND

Feet		Meters
12,000		4,000
9,000		3,000
6,000		2,000
4,500		1,500
3,000		1,000
1,200		400
600		200
0		0

▲ Mountain

HIMALAYA

Mt. Everest ▲
29,028 feet
(8,848 meters)

INDIA

Mountains on a Map

Mountains are easy to see on elevation maps. On these maps, different colors show different elevations. Different levels of a mountain from base to peak can often be seen.

Triangles on maps show single mountains. Usually, a mountain's name and elevation are shown beside the triangle.

Each year, many people use maps to climb and explore mountains. Mountains are one of earth's amazing landforms.

◀ A triangle shows Mount Everest's location. The light purple shows the high elevations of nearby mountains.

Glossary

climate (KLYE-mit)—the usual weather in a place

elevation (el-uh-VAY-shuhn)—the height above sea level; sea level is defined as zero elevation.

erode (i-RODE)—to wear away; wind and water erode soil and rock.

glacier (GLAY-shur)—a huge moving body of ice found in mountain valleys or polar regions

landslide (LAND-slide)—a sudden slide of earth and rocks down the side of a mountain

mountain range (MOUN-tuhn RAYNJ)—a large group or chain of mountains

peak (PEEK)—the pointed top of a mountain

tree line (TREE LINE)—the height on a mountain above which trees can't grow because of harsh weather conditions

Read More

Barnes, Julia. *101 Facts about Mountains.* 101 Facts about Our World. Milwaukee: Gareth Stevens, 2004.

Tidmarsh, Celia. *Mountains.* Geography First. San Diego: Blackbirch Press, 2004.

Internet Sites

FactHound offers a safe, fun way to find Internet sites related to this book. All of the sites on FactHound have been researched by our staff.

Here's how:
1. Visit *www.facthound.com*
2. Type in this special code **0736837140** for age-appropriate sites. Or enter a search word related to this book for a more general search.
3. Click on the **Fetch It** button.

FactHound will fetch the best sites for you!

Index